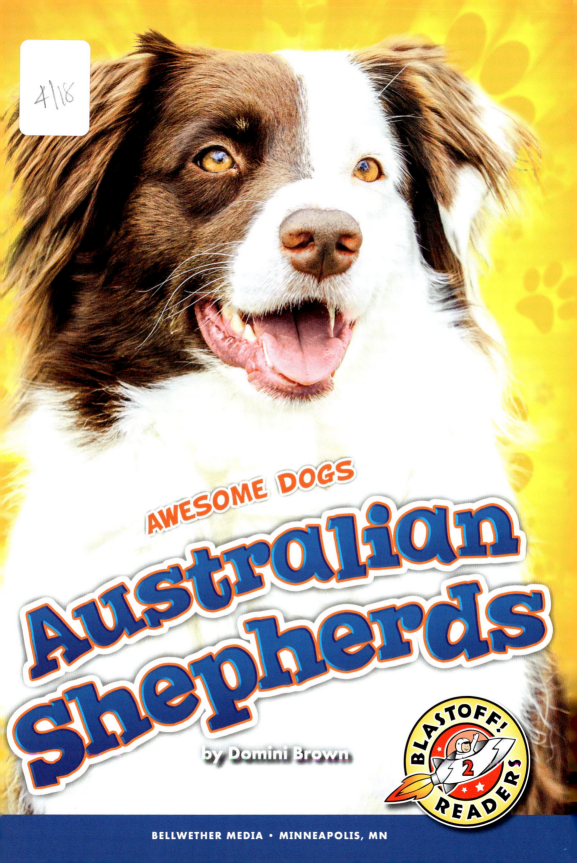

AWESOME DOGS

Australian Shepherds

by Domini Brown

BLASTOFF! READERS 2

BELLWETHER MEDIA • MINNEAPOLIS, MN

Note to Librarians, Teachers, and Parents:

Blastoff! Readers are carefully developed by literacy experts and combine standards-based content with developmentally appropriate text.

Level 1 provides the most support through repetition of high-frequency words, light text, predictable sentence patterns, and strong visual support.

Level 2 offers early readers a bit more challenge through varied simple sentences, increased text load, and less repetition of high-frequency words.

Level 3 advances early-fluent readers toward fluency through increased text and concept load, less reliance on visuals, longer sentences, and more literary language.

Level 4 builds reading stamina by providing more text per page, increased use of punctuation, greater variation in sentence patterns, and increasingly challenging vocabulary.

Level 5 encourages children to move from "learning to read" to "reading to learn" by providing even more text, varied writing styles, and less familiar topics.

Whichever book is right for your reader, Blastoff! Readers are the perfect books to build confidence and encourage a love of reading that will last a lifetime!

This edition first published in 2017 by Bellwether Media, Inc.

No part of this publication may be reproduced in whole or in part without written permission of the publisher. For information regarding permission, write to Bellwether Media, Inc., Attention: Permissions Department, 5357 Penn Avenue South, Minneapolis, MN 55419.

Library of Congress Cataloging-in-Publication Data

Title: Australian Shepherds / by Domini Brown.
Other titles: Blastoff! Readers. 2, Awesome Dogs.
Description: Minneapolis, MN : Bellwether Media, Inc., 2017. | Series:
   Blastoff! Readers. Awesome Dogs | Audience: Ages 5-8. | Audience:
   K to grade 3. | Includes bibliographical references and index.
Identifiers: LCCN 2015049297 | ISBN 9781626173910 (hardcover : alk. paper)
Subjects: LCSH: Australian shepherd dog–Juvenile literature. | Dog
   breeds–Juvenile literature.
Classification: LCC SF429.A79 B76 2017 | DDC 636.737–dc23
LC record available at http://lccn.loc.gov/2015049297

Printed in the United States of America, North Mankato, MN.

Table of Contents

What Are Australian Shepherds?

Australian shepherds are smart dogs. They like to learn new things.

They also love to play with their owners. Many people call them Aussies for short.

Aussies have two main **coat** patterns. These are **tri-color** and **merle**.

Australian Shepherd Coats

tri-color

merle

Coats are mostly red, black, or blue. They may have tan or white markings.

The **breed** has medium-length hair. It can be straight or wavy.

The hair on their legs is **feathered**. Soft manes hang from their necks.

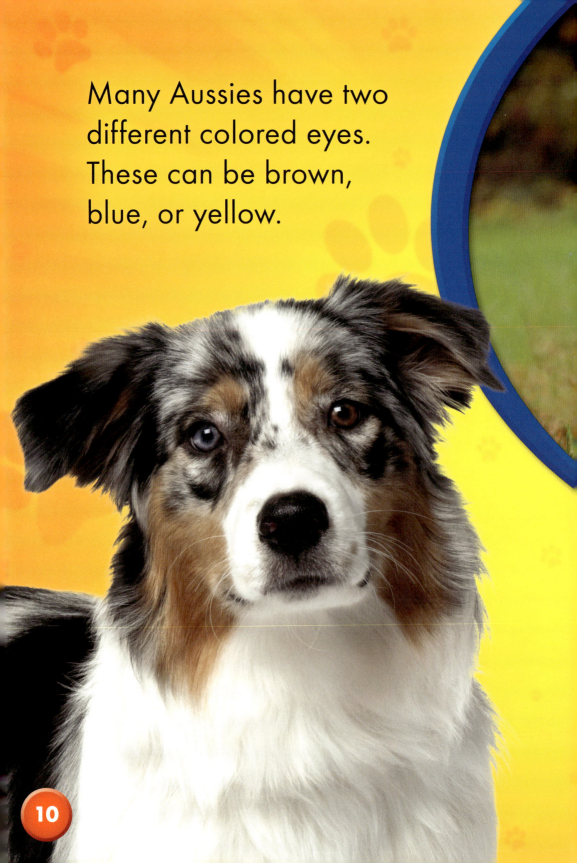

Many Aussies have two different colored eyes. These can be brown, blue, or yellow.

Many Aussies also have naturally **bobbed** tails.

History of Australian Shepherds

The breed began in the western United States during the 1800s.

United States

N
W E
S

People **bred** Aussies to work on farms and ranches. They proved to be excellent herding dogs.

In the 1950s, Aussies grew even more popular. They performed in **rodeos** and movies!

Australian Shepherd Profile

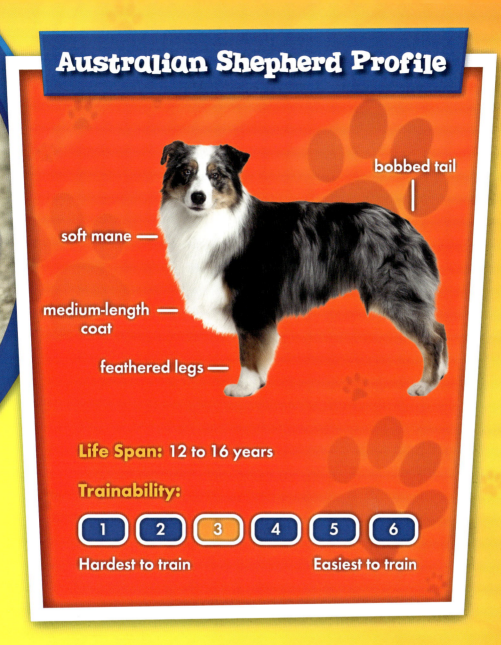

bobbed tail

soft mane —

medium-length — coat

feathered legs —

Life Span: 12 to 16 years

Trainability:

| 1 | 2 | 3 | 4 | 5 | 6 |

Hardest to train   Easiest to train

The medium-sized breed is in the **Herding Group** of the **American Kennel Club**.

Aussies are a true working breed. They need jobs to stay well-mannered.

Working helps use up Aussies' endless energy!

Some Australian shepherds are trained to be **guide dogs**.

Others work on **search and rescue** teams. They can work long hours.

These dogs also love fun activities.
They jump for Frisbees and race
in **agility**.

Aussies are happiest when their tongues hang out!

Glossary

agility—a dog sport in which dogs run through a series of obstacles

American Kennel Club—an organization that keeps track of dog breeds in the United States

bobbed—short and rounded

bred—purposely mated two dogs to make puppies with certain qualities

breed—a type of dog

coat—the hair or fur covering an animal

feathered—having longer hair on an animal's ears, legs, or tail

guide dogs—dogs trained to help blind people perform everyday tasks

Herding Group—a group of dog breeds that like to control the movement of other animals

merle—a pattern that is one solid color with patches and spots of another color

rodeos—contests and events in which people ride horses and bulls

search and rescue—teams that look for and help people in danger

tri-color—a pattern that has three colors

To Learn More

AT THE LIBRARY

Feiffer, Kate. *Henry the Dog with No Tail.* New York, N.Y.: Simon & Schuster Books for Young Readers, 2007.

Gunderson, Megan M. *Australian Shepherds.* Minneapolis, Minn.: ABDO Pub., 2013.

Hoffman, Mary Ann. *Herding Dogs.* New York, N.Y.: Gareth Stevens Pub., 2011.

ON THE WEB

Learning more about Australian shepherds is as easy as 1, 2, 3.

1. Go to www.factsurfer.com.

2. Enter "Australian shepherds" into the search box.

3. Click the "Surf" button and you will see a list of related web sites.

With factsurfer.com, finding more information is just a click away.

Index